# LESSONS FROM JOSHUA

SEE. TRUST. GO AND TAKE HOLD.

BRENNA KATE SIMONDS

Unveiled Faces Press

*Lessons from Joshua*

© 2024 by Brenna Kate Simonds

All rights reserved.

ISBN: 978-0-9911366-2-9

Unless otherwise noted, all Scripture references are taken from the Holy Bible, NEW INTERNATIONAL VERSION®. Copyright © 1973, 1978, 1984, 2011 by Biblica, Inc. All rights reserved worldwide. Used by permission.

Scripture quotations marked (ESV) are from The ESV® Bible (The Holy Bible, English Standard Version®), © 2001 by Crossway, a publishing ministry of Good News Publishers. Used by permission. All rights reserved.

Scriptures marked KJV are taken from the KING JAMES VERSION (KJV): KING JAMES VERSION, public domain.

Scriptures marked ASV are taken from the AMERICAN STANDARD VERSION (ASV): AMERICAN STANDARD VERSION, public domain.

Scripture quotations marked (NASB) are taken from the New American Standard Bible®, Copyright © 1960, 1962, 1963, 1968, 1971, 1972, 1973, 1975, 1977, 1995, 2011 by The Lockman Foundation. Used by permission.

Scripture quotations marked (NLT) are taken from the Holy Bible, New Living Translation, copyright © 1996, 2004, 2007, 2015 by Tyndale House Foundation. Used by permission of Tyndale House Publishers, Inc., Carol Stream, Illinois 60188. All rights reserved.

Scripture quotations marked (TLB) are taken from The Living Bible. Copyright ©1997, 1971 by Tyndale House Publishers, Inc. Used by permission. All rights reserved.

Copyediting and proofreading services by Sarah Geringer

Cover Design by Roy V. Simonds III

# CONTENTS

| | |
|---|---|
| Introduction | 1 |
| Background | 4 |
| 1. See. Trust. Go & Take Hold. | 11 |
| 2. Stepping into Your Jordan | 16 |
| 3. Stones of Remembrance | 21 |
| 4. Seeing with God's Eyes | 25 |
| 5. When Life Doesn't Make Sense | 29 |
| 6. Trust God to Care for You | 33 |
| 7. "But They Did Not Consult the Lord..." | 37 |
| 8. The Strength of Caleb | 41 |
| 9. God's Specific Plan | 45 |
| 10. Embrace Discomfort | 49 |
| 11. No Other Gods | 53 |
| 12. Choose for Yourself | 57 |
| Afterword: His Treasured Possession | 61 |
| Acknowledgements | 65 |
| *Notes* | 67 |

# INTRODUCTION

Has God ever given you a dream? I don't mean a "If only I could win a million dollars" dream. I'm not so sure those kinds of dreams are God-given. I mean a "deep down in your soul," "something only God could do" kind of dream.

Perhaps it's a dream for a loved one to be set free from addiction.

Maybe it's a dream for a life free from worry.

Or freedom from a mountain of debt.

Maybe you dream of a life without so many suffocating, negative thoughts.

It's difficult – even impossible – for you to imagine your dream coming true. You can clearly see all the obstacles; they line up like a wall made out of boulders right in front of you. You cannot see your way around them, and you cannot even begin to envision any way through them.

Joshua had a dream. It was a "deep down in your soul," "something only God could do" kind of dream. It was a dream God gave him decades before.

*Take My people into the Promised Land.*

This dream was originally given to Abraham. Hundreds of years before, God made an oath to Abraham that Israel would possess the land of the Canaanites. Abraham was 99 years old at the time and had no children with his wife Sarah. Yet God speaks to him in Genesis 17:8, "The whole land of Canaan, where you now reside as a foreigner, I will give as an everlasting possession to you and your descendants after you; and I will be their God." Abraham had a son Isaac who had twin boys Jacob and Esau. Jacob then had twelve sons whose descendants became known as the 12 tribes of Israel.

Hundreds of years went by, and the Israelites were enslaved in Egypt. God raised up a deliverer – Moses! You are likely familiar with pieces of this story. Ten plagues came, the Israelites left Egypt only to encounter the Red Sea, which God parted before them. The Egyptians, in hot pursuit of their work force, tried to follow them into the parted waters, only to be engulfed once the Israelites crossed over. The Israelites rejoiced in song over this great victory! Then they slowly allowed the hardships of the journey to cloud their memory of what God was able to do. Because of this, they remained in the wilderness until the older generation died out.

That would take 40 years. For four decades, Joshua (and the rest of the Israelites) wandered almost aimlessly through the wilderness on a journey that should have taken 11 days (Deuteronomy 1:2-3). For 40 years, I imagine Joshua dreamed, trusted, maybe even doubted, then dreamed and trusted again. For well over 14,000 days (instead of 11), Joshua tried to remember God's promise, to trust in who God is, and to believe that there was life beyond this wilderness wandering.

Throughout this book, I will do a lot of interpreting what we know about Joshua in order to give you a mental picture of how Joshua thinks and feels. This is a Bible study technique I have always used in an effort to more fully understand the text: draw together many things you know for sure in order to imagine the possibilities we cannot. I don't claim to fully know what it was like to be in Joshua's shoes (or sandals).Therefore, I encourage you to read the passages listed yourself in order to join me in learning these Lessons from Joshua.

Enter into a journey with me, Joshua, Moses and the Israelites. Together, let's feel the spray of the flooded Jordan on our faces and then stare at the city walls of Jericho. Let's watch the Israelites wrestle with trusting God, knowing that the same battle Joshua had to push through often lives in our own hearts. Most importantly, I want us to watch God. Let's see the obstacles before us with God's eyes. Let's trust Him in the midst of victories, struggles and triumphs. Then, as Joshua did, let's go and take hold of all He has for us. Let's enter into the story, realizing it's not just their story – it's our story, too.

# BACKGROUND

Let me get through some background before we dive into the book of the Bible entitled "Joshua." Please don't just skip this part! It's important and will really help you enter into and understand more thoroughly Joshua's life and the Israelites' experience.

Joshua first appears on the scene in Exodus 17. Without any prior reference or mention, Moses tells Joshua to choose the men who will fight the first battle that the Israelites encounter since leaving Egypt and heading toward the Promised Land. You may be familiar with the story because as the Israelites battle for victory, Moses says he will be standing "on top of the hill with the staff of God in my hands" (Exodus 17:9). As Joshua and his men fight the Amalekites, Moses held up his hands. When his hands dropped, the Amalekites began to win. Then, Moses's brother Aaron and a man named Hur gave Moses a stone to sit on and held up his hands "so that his hands remained steady till sunset. So Joshua overcame the Amalekite army with the sword" (Exodus 17:12b-13).

All we know about Joshua at this point is that he left Egypt with the Israelites and that he is apparently a warrior and leader in battle. But God knows everything about Joshua – his beginning and his end, his calling and his destiny. Just like God would later speak to Jeremiah:

> "Before I formed you in the womb I knew you,
> before you were born I set you apart." Jeremiah 1:5a

God knew exactly what He would call Joshua to do. For this reason, He needed Joshua to remember what had happened on the battlefield that day.

> "Then the Lord said to Moses, 'Write this on a scroll as something to be remembered *and make sure that Joshua hears it*, because I will completely blot out the name of Amalek from under heaven'" (Exodus 17:14), emphasis mine.

Moses may not have even known why he was making a record of this victory, but God knew.

Joshua would not be mentioned again until Exodus 24.

> "Then Moses set out with Joshua his aide, and Moses went up on the mountain of God" (Exodus 24:13).

Later in Numbers 11:28, it states that Joshua was "Moses' aide since youth." Other translations call Joshua "assistant" (ESV) or "personal servant" (NASB), even "minister" (ASV). The implication in Exodus 24 is that Joshua stayed on a lower part of the mountain, but it was likely a great comfort to Moses to have him nearby.

The final verse in Exodus mentioning Joshua concerns the tent of meeting, a place Moses created outside the camp to meet with God.

> "Now Moses used to take a tent and pitch it outside the camp some distance away, calling it 'the tent of meeting.' Anyone inquiring of the Lord would go to the tent of meeting outside

the camp. And whenever Moses went out to the tent, all the people rose and stood at the entrances to their tents, watching Moses until he entered the tent. As Moses went into the tent, the pillar of cloud would come down and stay at the entrance, while the Lord spoke with Moses. Whenever the people saw the pillar of cloud standing at the entrance to the tent, they all stood and worshiped, each at the entrance to their tent" (Exodus 33:7-10).

The Tent of Meeting was where people sought God. When Moses was there, the people would worship God from afar. It's as if they recognized the holiness of those moments but were afraid to venture away from the doors of their own homes toward the Tent of Meeting.

Not Joshua.

"The Lord would speak to Moses face to face, as one speaks to a friend. Then Moses would return to the camp, but his young aide Joshua son of Nun did not leave the tent" (Exodus 33:11).

Did Joshua know he had a call on his life of this magnitude? He worked closely with Moses from a young age. It wasn't until long after these moments at the Tent of Meeting that God would tell Moses he could not enter the Promised Land. Did Moses know he was training his replacement?

It's interesting to note that Joshua's name was once Hoshea. At some point, Hoshea son of Nun was given a new name by Moses: Joshua (Numbers 13:16). Most commentators agree that "Hoshea" means salvation and Joshua (the Greek form of which is "Jesus") means "God is salvation."[1] We don't know when this happened, but I imagine the significance was not lost on Joshua. He saw God's might and power when God sent plagues on Egypt, parted the Red Sea, and delivered the Israelites in battle. Was Joshua also hoping to hear from God directly himself?

I envision him lingering at the tent, just wanting to meet with God. To experience Him intimately, to hear His voice. Face to face, like Moses did.

Joshua may not have always understood that God wanted to meet with him personally. He may have thought that meeting with God and receiving from God was reserved for other people, people like Moses.

In Numbers 11, the people were complaining about manna. Manna was the food God gave them to eat while they were traveling to the Promised Land. Every day except the Sabbath, this manna would miraculously appear for them to eat (they collected a double portion the day before the Sabbath). Moses then cried out to God about this group of complaining people, even asking why God gave him "the job of nursing them along like babies" (v. 12, TLB). God then directed Moses to take the seventy leaders of Israel to the Tabernacle, and He would put the Spirit that was on Moses on the elders as well, so that the burden of the people would be shared.

The Lord did as He said. His Spirit rested on the elders at the tent, and they prophesied.

> "However, two men, whose names were Eldad and Medad, had remained in the camp. They were listed among the elders, but did not go out to the tent. Yet the Spirit also rested on them, and they prophesied in the camp. A young man ran and told Moses, 'Eldad and Medad are prophesying in the camp.'
>
> "Joshua son of Nun, who had been Moses' aide since youth, spoke up and said, 'Moses, my lord, stop them!'
>
> "But Moses replied, 'Are you jealous for my sake? I wish that all the Lord's people were prophets and that the Lord would put his Spirit on them!'" (Numbers 11:26-29)

Did this plant a seed in Joshua's mind? *Wait – others can have what Moses has? To have God's Spirit guiding them and speaking through them? Others, like maybe even me someday?* So he hovered. He waited outside the tent, longing to experience more of God for himself.

Just a short time later, Joshua was sent with 11 others to explore the land of Canaan, which God said, "I am giving to the Israelites" (Numbers 13:2). You may remember how that turned out! Most of the 12 spies were terrified of the people there. Caleb alone initially spoke up, stating, "We should go up and take possession of the land, for we can certainly do it," to which the rest replied, "We can't attack those people; they are stronger than we are" (v. 31). As if that wasn't enough, they then began to spread a "bad report" among the people, declaring, "the land we explored devours those living in it" (v. 32).

In Numbers 14, everything seems to fall apart. The Israelites even declare they should find a new leader to take them back to Egypt (v.4)! While Moses and Aaron fall facedown before the people, Joshua and Caleb declare, "The land we passed through and explored is exceedingly good. If the Lord is pleased with us, he will lead us into that land, a land flowing with milk and honey, and will give it to us. Only do not rebel against the Lord. And do not be afraid of the people of the land, because we will devour them. Their protection is gone, but the Lord is with us. Do not be afraid of them" (v. 7-9).

Caleb and Joshua state in faith that the land will not devour them, but that the Israelites will devour the land. Verse 9 as rendered in the NLT declares, "They are only helpless prey to us!"

But the people were not convinced; they even spoke of stoning Caleb and Joshua.

The other ten spies died due to their rebellion, and the people eventually realized their mistake and mourned. The Lord replied, "Not one of you will enter the land I swore with uplifted hand to make your home, except Caleb son of Jephunneh and Joshua son of Nun. As for your children that you said would be taken as plunder, I will bring them in to enjoy the land you have rejected" (Numbers 14:30-31).

While the Israelites then wandered in the wilderness for 40 years, God had not forgotten His words to Joshua, that he would see the Promised Land. For 40 years, God had been preparing Joshua. When the years of wandering were coming to a close, it was time to call out of Joshua what God knew was always there.

> "So the Lord said to Moses, 'Take Joshua son of Nun, a man in whom is the spirit of leadership, and lay your hand on him. Have him stand before Eleazar the priest and the entire assembly and commission him in their presence. Give him some of your authority so the whole Israelite community will obey him. He is to stand before Eleazar the priest, who will obtain decisions for him by inquiring of the Urim before the Lord. At his command he and the entire community of the Israelites will go out, and at his command they will come in.'"
>
> "Moses did as the Lord commanded him. He took Joshua and had him stand before Eleazar the priest and the whole assembly. Then he laid his hands on him and commissioned him, as the Lord instructed through Moses" (Numbers 27:18-23).

At the end of every section, there will be a prayer. Feel free to pray it to yourself, pray it out loud, or pray in your own words.

*Prayer: Lord, that was a lot of information on Joshua! One thing that sticks out is Joshua hovering at the tent. Lord, let me draw close to You. Help me to learn from You, from this book, and from the lives of those who seek after You with their whole hearts. Lord, let me cling to You as Joshua did. Let me not reject what You have in store for me as the Israelites did, but let me trust You to carry me into the Promised Land, whatever that may look like. I pray this in Jesus' mighty name. Amen.*

# 1

## SEE. TRUST. GO & TAKE HOLD.

*Suggested Scripture Reading: Deuteronomy 1*

Has anyone ever given you a gift that you didn't open? Maybe it was in a box with entirely too much tape on it. Full of anticipation, you began the process of tearing the tape off piece by piece, trying to figure out which piece was on top and which one to remove first. The excitement wore off when you realized the work ahead of you, and you put it aside for another day.

Perhaps you had an idea of what was in the box, a glimpse of the gift you would receive. While the idea of the gift was enticing, you weren't sure it was any better than what you already had. You could see the obstacles that stood in the way of what you were given, and they seemed insurmountable.

The idea is a bit silly but is so relevant to what is about to happen in the story. Before we jump into the Promised Land and into the book of Joshua, I want to focus for a moment on a directive that becomes a theme in Joshua.

The book of Deuteronomy is one long admonition from Moses to the Israelites. It is situated in the Bible directly before the book of Joshua. While this story is not in Joshua, the words in this book set the stage for what is to come. In Moses's final speech to the Israelites, I came upon this gem:

> "See, the Lord your God has given you the land. Go up and take possession of it" (Deuteronomy 1:21a).

This isn't just one passing comment. In fact, in the book of Deuteronomy, the new land is promised to the Israelites 69 times. Despite that, I can't help but imagine these people thinking, *God has given us the land? What? In what way and how?* All these people had known for 40 years was aimless wandering, but now they were supposed to somehow envision what God was planning to do?

Isn't this just like God? Later in the story, when Joshua is staring at the walled city of Jericho, it was so closed up that no one was even coming or going. Yet, what was God's perspective? God basically tells them, "See, I have delivered Jericho into your hands – now go and take it" (a summary of Joshua 6:2-5 which we will discuss more thoroughly later).

How did God direct the Israelites to enter the Promised Land? How does God ask the same of us?

First, God asks us to see. Not with our physical eyes, but our spiritual ones. Not with our own limited perspective, but with His unlimited perspective. The Israelites could not "see" how God could deliver them from slavery in Egypt, how they would get through the Red Sea, or how God was going to feed all of those people and provide water for them. God was asking them (and us) to see beyond what we can touch and hold, and envision what He is able to do. If He has said He will do it, then He will do it.

As we discussed, the Israelites sent spies in to scout out the land. All the spies reported that the land God would give them was indeed good land, even bringing back some fruit. They also reported that the people were stronger and taller than them, and the cities large and walled (Deut. 1:28). Rather than focus on what God asked them to see, they fixated on what they saw with their eyes. God wanted the Israelites to first see with His perspective.

Second, God asks us to trust. In Deuteronomy 1:30-31, God recounts how He fought for the Israelites in Egypt and in the wilderness. "There you saw how the Lord your God carried you, as a father carries his son, all the way you went until you reached this place" (v. 31). He continues, "In spite of this, you did not trust in the Lord your God" (v. 32).

God had promised a land flowing with milk and honey to the Israelites, into a land He promised that He would bring them. The Israelites simply needed to take God at His Word from this point forward. Even in times when what they saw didn't make sense, God asked them to trust in His promises instead of fixating on the fear in their hearts.

Third, God asks us to go and take hold. After deciding to see things through God's eyes, after choosing to trust in God, God then asks us, as He did the Israelites, to take a step of faith. He asks us to go and take hold of all that He has for us. The Israelites chose not to do this with disastrous consequences. Only Caleb and Joshua got to walk in the fullness of God's promises.

As believers in and followers of Jesus Christ, God has given us so much. In fact, He "has given us everything we need for a godly life" (2 Peter 1:3). Peter goes on to talk about God's "very great and precious promises, so that through them you may participate in the divine nature" (v. 4).

In typical God fashion, though, this too is something where we need to go and take hold. "For this very reason, make every effort to add to your faith goodness; and to goodness, knowledge; and to knowledge, self-control; and to self-control, perseverance; and to perseverance, godliness, and to godliness, mutual affection; and to mutual affection, love" (2 Peter 1:5-7).

Henry T. and Richard Blackaby share this concerning God's command to take possession of the Promised Land: "One of the paradoxes of the Christian life is that God's gifts often require labor on our part."[1] The apostle Paul knew this intimately when he wrote the following to the church in Philippi: "Not that I have already obtained all this, or have already arrived at my goal, but I press on to take hold of that for which Christ Jesus took hold of me. Brothers and sisters, I do not consider myself yet to have taken hold of it. But one thing I do: Forgetting what is behind and straining toward what is ahead, I press on toward the goal to win the prize for which God has called me heavenward in Christ Jesus" (Philippians 3:12-14).

This will be a theme for us as we travel through Joshua.

See.

Trust.

Go and take hold.

It wasn't just a command for the Israelites; it is a command for us today.

A brief comment: one thing I do not cover in this book is the place of war in going and taking hold of the Promised Land. I recognize this may be a difficult thing for some to understand. I have two suggestions here. First, pray. Ask God to open your eyes and your heart to the bigger story at work in the book of Joshua. Second, do some reading - elsewhere. I'm going to leave this topic to scholars and theologians far more qualified than I. It is beyond the scope of this book, but there are some resources in the footnotes.[2]

Is there a promise from God that you have not yet received? First, see with His eyes. Second, trust in His promises. Third, go and take hold.

"See, the Lord your God has given you the land. Go up and take possession of it as the Lord, the God of your fathers, told you. Do not be afraid; do not be discouraged" (Deuteronomy 1:21).

*Prayer: Father God, I generally spend my time focusing on what*

*I can see, which is often the obstacles and the challenges, or my own failures and flaws. I am reminded of Psalm 25:15: "My eyes are ever on the Lord, for only he will release my feet from the snare." Lord, help me first to take my eyes off the snare and look to You, asking for Your perspective. Second, help me to trust. Lord, I choose to trust – to believe You are who You say You are and You will do what You have said You will do. As I learn to see with Your eyes and trust in Your heart, empower me with the courage and strength only You can give to go and take hold of all that You have for me, in Your perfect timing. Thank You for always believing in me, not because of my own strengths, Lord, but because You see who You created me to be and You know all I can overcome if I choose to rely on You fully. It is because of Your Son Jesus Christ that I can pray these things. Amen.*

# 2

## STEPPING INTO YOUR JORDAN

*Suggested Scripture reading: Joshua 1, 3*

"Into the Wild" is a biographical sketch of the story of Christopher McCandless as written by Jon Krakauer.[1]

In 1990, Christopher McCandless, a young man in his 20's, set out on a cross-country journey to explore the unexplored and experience life without responsibilities. After two years on the road, McCandless crossed a small river in a remote area of Alaska and ended up living in an abandoned bus he came across. He stayed here for a few months, but he soon tired of gathering his own food in the harsh reality of living alone in the wild.

When McCandless wanted to return to his friends and family, he found that the river which he crossed in snowy April had become wide, deep, and violent due to the thaw, thus making it impossible to cross. In the story, it seems as if time stands still. McCandless stopped there, perfectly silent, and stared at the wild river that made him a prisoner of his choices.

We are in the beginning of Joshua. The first chapter is full of powerful promises to Joshua and the Israelites. Here are a few:

"I will give you every place where you set your foot, as I promised Moses" (v. 3).

"No one will be able to stand against you all the days of your life. As I was with Moses, so I will be with you; I will never leave you nor forsake you" (v. 5).

Here is perhaps the most well-known verse in Joshua:

"Have I not commanded you? Be strong and courageous. Do not be afraid; do not be discouraged, for the Lord your God will be with you wherever you go" (v. 9).

What powerful words! What precious promises! If this were a pep rally, I'd be all riled up, ready to take on my opponent!

The story continues in Joshua 1:

"So Joshua ordered the officers of the people: 'Go through the camp and tell the people, 'Get your provisions ready. Three days from now you will cross the Jordan here to go in and take possession of the land the Lord your God is giving you for your own'" (v. 10-11).

Imagine that you are in the shoes of the Israelites. In Joshua 2, we have the story of the two spies looking over the land, and Rahab hiding the spies. The spies return from Jericho with this report: "The LORD has surely given the whole land into our hands; all the people are melting in fear because of us" (v. 24). There was likely much celebration! After 40 years of their ancestors wandering in the wilderness, the Israelites would finally see the Promised Land.

Soon after, the Israelites were instructed to pack up their things and move their camp to the banks of the Jordan River (Joshua 3:1).

In one of my readings of this story, a detail I had never noticed leapt out at me.

"Now the Jordan is at flood stage all during harvest" (Joshua 3:15).

Put yourself in their tents for a minute. For three days, they camped near the river's edge. Imagine the spray from the flooded river, with the violent water vigorously lapping the banks. Almost all of them had never even been around a major body of water before. They must have been thinking through all the possibilities of how they would get across as they stared at the obstacle that stood between them and their dreams of a better life.

*Perhaps a boat would work? How long will it take us to build boats for a million people? What about the children, the livestock, all our possessions?*

There would have been a few who remembered crossing the Red Sea as children or young people, and others who heard the story from their elders. Could God do something like that again?

At the end of the third day, Joshua commanded them, "Consecrate yourselves, for tomorrow the LORD will do amazing things among you" (v. 5). The anticipation grew. The next morning, everyone awoke and prepared to move forward. The people were directed to follow the Ark of the Covenant at a distance, while the priests were commanded: "When you reach the edge of the Jordan's waters, go and stand in the river" (v. 8).

When the Red Sea parted, the waters had already been divided prior to the Israelites stepping into the newly created dry land. Why wasn't God going to do that again? Was He examining or testing them, as if to make sure they were really on board? The Israelites wandered in the wilderness because of their disobedience and hard hearts. Why was He requiring an extra act of faith on the part of the priests, that they should step directly into the flood waters they had been watching for three days? Was He in essence, saying, "This is it, guys. We're almost there. Are you going to continue to see with My eyes, choose to trust, and go and take hold?"

John Ortberg calls this "the first step principle."[2] It usually begins with me acting in faith—trusting God enough to take a step of obedience. Simply acknowledging information about his power is not enough. I have to get my feet wet. But when I say yes, I set in motion an adventure that will leave me forever changed."

They had to get their feet wet first. The priests, in obedience to God's command, stepped out into the flood waters. They had the Ark of the Covenant, a sign of God's presence and His promises, with them. If God didn't do something miraculous, they would be swept away.

The water piled up in a heap beside them, and there the priests stood, in the middle of the river on dry ground, waiting until all of Israel was safely on the other side, witnessing God's faithfulness.

What is your Jordan?

What is the thing that is standing between you and your dreams, your freedom, and the Promised Land to which God is calling you? The thing that feels insurmountable to you?

Are you standing on the banks of your Jordan, as Christopher McCandless did on that river's edge in Alaska, overwhelmed by the cold spray on your face and the rushing waters at your feet? Are you staring at the river, the obstacle in your way, positive that you, like him, are destined to be a prisoner of your past choices?

If you are a believer in and follower of Jesus Christ, you are no longer a prisoner of anything but righteousness (Romans 6:18). The amazing thing about the God we serve is that He sets the captives free, and He brings us from darkness into light. If He is calling you to step out, He will make a way where there seems to be no way (Isaiah 61:1, Ephesians 5:8, Isaiah 43:16-19).

Are you willing to see your Jordan but still take that first step as the Israelites did? Will you choose to trust that God has gone ahead of you, and that He is able to help you go and take hold?

*Prayer: Lord God, it's hard for me to trust sometimes when all I see is the Jordan River, overflowing, menacing, and powerful. But You, the God who spared no expense in His rescue mission of me, are even more powerful than any obstacle I perceive; Your provision and presence overflow all around me. Lord, help me trust that if I take the first step, as John Ortberg said, "I set in motion an adventure that will leave me forever changed." Lord, I desperately want to be changed. I want to be made new. I don't want to live in fear. No matter the obstacles, I commit to step into the water when I hear Your voice calling me – because You have empowered me to do so. I pray in the name of Your Son who gave His life so that I might live. Amen.*

# 3

# STONES OF REMEMBRANCE

*Suggested Scripture reading: Joshua 4*

The Israelites had just crossed the Jordan. They had seen God's hand move powerfully and faithfully, as He continued to do what He had promised He would do.

Then God told Joshua to choose one man from each tribe for a special task.

"So Joshua called together the twelve men he had appointed from the Israelites, one from each tribe, and said to them, "Go over before the ark of the LORD your God into the middle of the Jordan. Each of you is to take up a stone on his shoulder, according to the number of the tribes of the Israelites, to serve as a sign among you. In the future, when your children ask you, 'What do these stones mean?' tell them that the flow of the Jordan was cut off before the ark of the covenant of the LORD. When it crossed the Jordan, the waters of the Jordan were cut off. These stones are to be a memorial to the people of Israel forever" (Joshua 4:4-7).

Why didn't God tell them to get the stones on their way through the river? Is this again another little faith test, like when He commanded them to step into the flooded river, and only then would the waters part? While crossing the river, the Israelites were specifically instructed to stay a half mile away from the Ark of the Covenant, whereas now they are told to gather rocks from where the priests are standing. The stones needed to be from the very spot where the Ark of the Covenant, a sign of God's presence and His promises, was held.

Notice they weren't celebratory stones. It would have been a fine time to celebrate, but no. The "Stones of Remembrance" served as a memorial.

We often think of memorials as a way to remember someone who has died, but more often they are a way to remind people of a person or event.[1] In this case, they built a memorial to God's faithfulness. It served as a reminder that His promises were, and still are, true. It was a reminder that an era of slavery and wilderness wanderings had ended. It reminded them that there would be a new beginning in the Promised Land.

Why did they need this memorial? The reality of life is that we all get discouraged. "Discouraged" is really too weak of a word – "disheartened" is better. Proverbs 13:12a says, "Hope deferred makes the heart sick." We get hyper-focused on our vision of how things should be. We may even have a picture of how, when, and why God will show up and come through for us. Yet our focus gets sidetracked by the wait. We seem to forget all that God is and quickly lose sight of all He has done in us and through us.

The Israelites certainly had a preconceived idea of how God's deliverance should look. Imagine the Israelites, enslaved for 400 years. For all those generations, they spent their days, dreaming of how God would show up, while subject to the whims of Pharaoh. In my article "Craving Egypt," I write about how quickly the Israelites lost sight of all that God had done to deliver them from slavery.[2] The following words were spoken by the Israelites soon after the parting of the Red Sea.

"If only we had died by the Lord's hand in Egypt! There we sat around pots of meat and ate all the food we wanted, but you have brought us out into this desert to starve this entire assembly to death" (Exodus 16:3).

The Stones of Remembrance after the crossing of the Jordan served not just as a reminder, but also as a warning. You will forget. You will lose sight. You will get off kilter, lose focus, and sink into despair. You will even come up with your own ideas of what freedom looks like and how it should arrive.

It's as if God is saying: *I've carried you this far. Trust Me. I'm not going to stop caring for you now. It may not look like you think it will, but I am still here and I am still working.*

The Stones of Remembrance encourage us to focus on the "who" rather than the "how." This is hard because we really love the "how"! We love imagining and conjuring up the grand scheme of how God is going to work in a particular situation. We're not so enthusiastic about simply resting in the knowledge of who God is and choosing to trust Him. We get too caught up in the details of the "how" to remember to fix our eyes on the "who": the eternal presence of Jesus.

We too can gather Stones of Remembrance: times God came through, often in surprising ways.

At a former residence, I had a bulletin board in my office next to my desk. I would stick things there to remind me of God's faithfulness. One such thing was a mask from when one of my kids had surgery, a reminder of how God showed His care for me and my son in answering a very specific prayer of mine. These days, in the back of my journal, I write down the times when God has shown up in big and small ways, times I really felt His care, even when my faith was small.

Start writing it down. Look back through your journals,

your emails, your Facebook status updates, and start a new journal. Write down the date and the way in which God came through, the manner in which He reminded you that He is good. Note the person through whom He spoke truth, the way He miraculously provided, and the Scripture you heard three times in the same week.

Write it down. You will forget. You will lose sight. We all do.

"And he [Joshua] said to the sons of Israel, "When your children ask their fathers in time to come, saying, 'What are these stones?' then you shall inform your children, saying, 'Israel crossed this Jordan on dry ground.' For the Lord your God dried up the waters of the Jordan before you until you had crossed, just as the Lord your God had done to the Red Sea, which He dried up before us until we had crossed; so that all the peoples of the earth may know that the hand of the Lord is mighty, so that you may fear the Lord your God forever" (Joshua 4:21-24, NLT).

That's why we, like the Israelites, need Stones of Remembrance. They are what we reach for when we are disheartened, weighed down by the burden of problems we were never meant to carry alone. They remind us of God's faithfulness, of His power, and that we can trust in Him.

*Prayer: Lord, forgive me that my vision is so limited, my heart is so fickle, and my memory is so inconsistent. Forgive me for becoming disheartened so quickly after seeing You come through for me. Help me, like the Israelites, to set up Stones of Remembrance. Let them be memorials of Your faithfulness and reminders of Your goodness, pointing me back to Your promises. Help me remember that You have always been faithful, and You will be faithful again. In Jesus' name I pray, Amen*

## 4

## SEEING WITH GOD'S EYES

*Suggested Scripture reading: Joshua 5-6*

The Israelites had just stepped into the Jordan, crossed it, and taken up their Stones of Remembrance. Joshua circumcised the Israelites.[1] They healed and rested, and then celebrated the Passover (Joshua 5:3, 8, 10). The day after the Passover, the Israelites ate some of the produce from the land, and the manna stopped (v. 11-12).

> "Now it came about when Joshua was by Jericho, he raised his eyes and looked, and behold, a man was standing opposite him with his sword drawn in his hand, and Joshua went to him and said to him, 'Are you for us or for our enemies?' He said, 'No; rather I have come now *as* captain of the army of the LORD.' And Joshua fell on his face to the ground, and bowed down, and said to him, 'What has my lord to say to his servant?' And the captain of the LORD's army said to Joshua, 'Remove your sandals from your feet, for the place where you are standing is holy.' And Joshua did so." (Joshua 5:13-15, NASB).

Many commentators on this passage believe that the commander of the army of the LORD was Jesus Himself. The Tyndale commentary states, "In the light of the covenantal requirements that only the LORD God should be worshipped (cf. Exod. 20 and Deut. 5-8), there can be no doubt who this is."[2] Matthew Henry notes, "We read not of any appearance of God's glory to Joshua till now."[3] Joshua worshipped Him & referred to Him as "my Lord."

Prior to this time, God had been speaking directly to Joshua, over and over again. He had not bodily appeared to Joshua, nor had an angel visited him. Why, then, did Joshua need God Himself to come speak to him face to face?

Notice that Joshua was near his next obstacle when the above happened. What he was thinking? Was he staring at the obstacle, wondering how they could ever overcome it? I imagine him standing there, reminding himself of who his deliverer was, and remembering that memorial of stones. In that moment, the Scripture says that Joshua "lifted up his eyes" (v. 13, ESV).

I wonder if Joshua was a little hesitant to take on the task of leading the Israelites into the Promised Land. It was monumental. Joshua clearly revered Moses, who left some big shoes to fill. While Moses bargained with God about whether or not he would make a good leader (Exodus 4), Joshua seemed to accept his role more willingly, without negotiation. Yet over and over in Joshua 1, God reminds him to be strong and courageous and to not be afraid.

This man, the commander of the Lord's army, came as commander in chief before the Israelites first big battle in the Promised Land, with sword drawn. He appeared as a soldier to encourage another solider, to share a holy moment before the battles to come.

Then the story, with no transition, jumps right into what is happening at Jericho, the very thing Joshua was pondering prior to the visitation of the glory of the Lord. "Now the gates of

Jericho were securely barred because of the Israelites. No one went out and no one came in. Then the LORD said to Joshua, 'See, I have delivered Jericho into your hands, along with its king and its fighting men'" (Joshua 6:1-2).

You are likely quite familiar with this story and the strange instructions God gave to Joshua and the Israelites concerning how exactly to conquer Jericho. If you're not familiar, please go and read Joshua 6:1-7. I remember reading this myself many years ago and thinking, *Huh? That doesn't even make sense!* To the natural eye, Jericho was shut up, snug as a bug in a rug, with high walls and no way in. The story clearly states that no one was even coming or going. But what was God's perspective? He says, "See." It's as if God said to Joshua, *Look at this with My eyes. I have already delivered this city into your hands.*

In our everyday lives, it seems easier to take things at face value, envisioning obstacles as insurmountable and struggles as unconquerable. But the reality of following Jesus is you and I have already been set free from the laws of sin and death. In fact, you've already been set free from that struggle that just came to mind as you doubted the truth in this paragraph. In that situation you are looking at, the one that seems perfectly hopeless, God is saying, *Consecrate yourself to Me. I already have a plan to be glorified. I will deliver you from that thing that has you bound. I can do the miraculous in the midst of that hopeless situation. Look at this with My eyes.*

Are you speaking truth to yourself concerning your troubling situation and the obstacles you are facing? Are you placing your hope in all the ways you have conjured up to possibly fix it, or all the probable outcomes you've imagined? Or are you hoping in the power of God, the same God who parted the Jordan, and brought down the mighty walls of Jericho?

Because hopelessness was a huge struggle for me in my early days of walking with Jesus, I memorized these verses early on:

"Therefore we do not lose heart. Though outwardly we are wasting away, yet inwardly we are being renewed day by day. For our light and momentary troubles are achieving for us an eternal glory that far outweighs them all. So we fix our eyes not on what is seen, but on what is unseen, since what is seen is temporary, but what is unseen is eternal" (2 Corinthians 4:16-18).

What we see (our struggles, circumstances, burdens, and obstacles) are not only light and momentary, but they are temporary in God's eyes. Read that again: this is temporary.

We have a choice: stare at the mighty walls of Jericho, or lift up our eyes to gaze upon our great God.

We know the end of this story. The walls fell because Joshua chose to look to his Creator, the Lover of his soul, his Deliverer. Because of Joshua's decision to lift his eyes, it seems as if God replied, "Since you chose to look to Me, I am about to do something amazing."

See.

Trust.

Go and take hold once again.

*Prayer: Oh, Lord, how often I stare at the walls of my Jericho. No one is coming or going, and it seems as if nothing is happening or could happen. But You see something very different! You see an opportunity to move and heal and encourage and just be God. I choose to look to You, the One who is able. I choose to trust in You, the God who sees me. I choose to rely on You, the One who is faithful. Do what only You can as only You can as You empower me to go and take hold. I pray in Jesus' name. Amen.*

## 5

## WHEN LIFE DOESN'T MAKE SENSE

*Suggested Scripture reading: Joshua 7*

After reading about God's great victory in Jericho, chapter 7 is slightly painful. Following stories of triumph and radical obedience on the way to the Promised Land, Israel loses its battle with Ai.

Joshua 7:1 begins with the ominous phrase, "But the Israelites were unfaithful in regard to the devoted things." The NASB states it this way: "But the sons of Israel acted unfaithfully regarding the things designated for destruction," better capturing the command from God in Joshua 6:18. I will dive into this command more thoroughly in the following chapter.

Joshua did not know that the Israelites had not all followed God's directive. After the victory in Jericho, Joshua sent men to spy on Ai, to see what was needed for their next battle. The spies advised that only about two or three thousand men must go fight Ai, because "only a few people live there" (Joshua 7:3). The men went up to fight Ai. However, the Israelites were quickly and sorely defeated, and "the hearts of the people melted in fear and became like water" (Joshua 7:5c).

Joshua was understandably upset. How could this have

happened? Joshua and the elders of Israel wisely went before the Lord to find out, praying and fasting until evening. The story continues:

> "And Joshua said, "Alas, Sovereign Lord, why did you ever bring this people across the Jordan to deliver us into the hands of the Amorites to destroy us? If only we had been content to stay on the other side of the Jordan! Pardon your servant, Lord. What can I say, now that Israel has been routed by its enemies? The Canaanites and the other people of the country will hear about this and they will surround us and wipe out our name from the earth. What then will you do for your own great name?'" (Joshua 7:7-9).

Before we dive into what exactly preceded this loss, let us first look at some lessons we can gather from Joshua's response to this surprising defeat.

1. **Ask God, "Why?"** Joshua immediately went before the Lord. He prayed, and he fasted. He tore his clothes, fell facedown, and begged God to answer his cries and pardon him. He knew that God alone can bring clarity. This seems to be the only time Joshua questions God in this manner. It's something we see from both Moses and the Israelites all throughout the book of Exodus and Numbers as I'll mention in the next point, but is not typical behavior for Joshua.

Often, we are told that good Christians do not question God. We are instructed to just accept His sovereignty and whatever He sends our way. While that can be good advice at times, there is also wisdom in finding out where we might have gone wrong.

King David in Psalm 139 prays, "Search me, God, and know my heart; test me and know my anxious thoughts. See if there is any offensive way in me, and lead me in the way everlasting" (Psalm 139:23-24). It is God's job to search our hearts and illuminate our faults and sins. James wrote, "If you need wisdom, ask our generous God, and he will give it to you. He will not rebuke you for asking" (James 1:5, NLT). If you need understanding about a situation in your life, ask for it. If God doesn't give you insight, then trust Him to guide you through it.

2. **Don't settle.** Joshua did go immediately before the Lord, but his prayer is eye-opening. Rather than simply asking God, "What happened?" he said, in essence, "Why did we ever cross the Jordan? This whole 'getting into the Promised Land' is too hard! Why didn't we just accept 'good enough'?"

Joshua spent decades in the wilderness. His traveling companions weren't exactly pillars of confidence and encouragement. "If only we never left Egypt!" they cried. Maybe Egypt was "good enough." After all, there were meat and melons there (Numbers 11:4-5).

Joshua's confidence in God's ability to give them victory was generally strong. That's why this defeat was such a shock to him and had him questioning God's direction. Perhaps Joshua was so happy to be out of slavery and out of the wilderness that he thought maybe the Israelites should have permanently made camp on the other side of the Jordan. It was, after all, "good enough."

But it wasn't God's perfect plan or His best.

We must choose not to settle for what appears to be good. As Oswald Chambers said, "The good is often the enemy of God's best."[1]

3. **Be prepared to act.** Verse 10 records God's directive, "Stand up! What are you doing down on your face?"

Joshua doubted for a moment the goodness of God's plan to bring the Israelites into the Promised Land. But God didn't let him stay in that place for very long. There is a time for prayer and mourning, and there is a time for action. There is a time for tearing our clothes (a metaphor for grief) and laying prostrate, and there is a time to make right what is wrong. Israel had sinned, as we learn in the following verse. It was now time for consecration of the people and a rededication to the Lord.

God wants us to align our priorities with His priorities. We need to ask, we can't settle, and then we must be prepared to act.

*Prayer: God, sometimes it seems as if life doesn't make sense. Help me to choose to trust You in the midst of it. When I ask for clarity, Lord, let me hear Your answer. Let me not settle for "good enough." May I have the discernment to know when to wait on You in prayer and when to take action. Let me see disappointments through Your eyes and with Your perspective. In Jesus' name I pray. Amen.*

# 6
# TRUST GOD TO CARE FOR YOU

*Suggested Scripture reading: Joshua 8*

For years and years, I didn't believe God would provide for me financially. From the early days of being married, we struggled to make ends meet. I had a steady job initially, which I left after six months to go into the ministry. I thought because I was doing God's work that we would be all set. Yet things were extremely lean. We lived in such a bad part of town that the electricity would go out regularly. They even stopped delivering mail for a while because there were so many shootings. Once someone asked if I lived there as a ministry assignment. His wording was rather rude, and I reply curtly, "We're poor," and left it at that.

My experience was complicated by the fact that during my childhood, there were times my emotional needs and even my physical needs were ignored. It can be more difficult to believe that God is going to provide for you when that has not been your experience with others who were charged with your care and nurture.

In Joshua 6, we read God's directives on how to handle what is found in Jericho. God's specific instructions included, "But keep away from the devoted things, so that you will not bring about your own destruction by taking any of them. Otherwise, you will make the camp of Israel liable to destruction and bring trouble on it" (v. 18). God goes on to state that the precious metals found in Jericho must be dedicated to the house of God, and that the Israelites are not to take anything they find. Everything else must be destroyed. Yet a man named Achan disobeyed and hid some things under his tent.

Given my own experience, I can certainly imagine the temptation the Israelites may have felt. *After my wilderness wanderings, wouldn't some of these beautiful items that Jericho offers fit wonderfully in my new home? Surely God would not mind if I took one or two things for myself? Did He really mean for me not to keep anything?*

The essence of these ponderings is, *Did God really say?* This was the very question that the serpent asked Eve in the garden (Genesis 3:1). Satan's choice of words inferred this: "Isn't God withholding something good from you?"

After telling Joshua to get up during his time of prayer, God instructed Joshua to go through all of the Israelites, tribe by tribe, clan by clan, and family by family, in order to discover who had disobeyed the Lord. I can only imagine this was a lengthy and excruciating process.

Once his family was chosen, Achan confessed in Joshua 7:21: "When I saw in the plunder a beautiful robe from Babylonia, two hundred shekels of silver and a bar of gold weighing fifty shekels, I coveted them and took them. They are hidden in the ground inside my tent, with the silver underneath." In that moment, Achan did not trust that God would have good things for his family in the Promised Land if he just obeyed God completely.

I personally watched God come through for me on many occasions. One exceptional example occurred within a few months of following God. I became a follower of Jesus in January of 1999. Within a month or two, I found out about tithing. Since I became a believer at the beginning of the year, I looked at my paystub and tithed on what I made so far (I was a student at the time and admittedly it wasn't a lot). Not long after, I received my updated financial aid statement for what would be my last year of college. In addition to a small scholarship I already received, I had been given several new grants and interest-free loans that would more than cover my last year of school. I wouldn't even need my father to co-sign another private loan to cover additional costs because there weren't any. I could not help but conclude that this tithing thing really worked! Yet there were many times, years down the road, that I doubted.

One of God's main directives to the Israelites as they prepared to leave the wilderness behind was that they continue to walk in obedience to His commandments. They would not be successful in the Promised Land if they did not choose to obey whatever God required of them, even if it didn't make sense to them at the time. They needed to really trust Him.

I heard someone say recently that Jericho is an example of the first fruits principle. God wants our best first. He wants our offering (a tithe of our income) first. It can't be an afterthought to be a worthy offering. Thus, God wanted the plunder from Jericho to first be an offering to Him. He was asking the Israelites to trust that they would receive their own blessings in due time.

For us today, giving a tithe to God means recognizing that everything God has blessed us with belongs to Him anyway.[1] Out of our gratitude, we give the first part of the blessing back to Him. It is also a way of demonstrating we trust that God is ultimately our provider, and that He will take care of us.

In Joshua 8, when Israelites attack Ai again, God allows the Israelites to "carry off their plunder and livestock for yourselves" (v. 2). Achan would have gotten some of those beautiful items for his new home, if he had just trusted that God would take care of him eventually.

You may not worry about money, but I'm fairly certain you can think of an area where you've worried whether God would come through in your life. God has never *not* provided for us – in every area. In the times of little and in the times of plenty, God has always been Jehovah Jireh – the Lord who provides. I've come to a place where I really believe that.

God wants our trust because He is trustworthy.

*Prayer: Lord, like Achan, I have struggled to believe that You will provide. I have coveted and envied what others have. I have looked at the grass on other lawns, so to speak, and it looks so much greener and lusher than mine. Help me to trust You. Help me to look back at those stones of remembrance and see all the times You have come through for me. You have been so good to me. Thank You that you clothe the flowers and feed the birds, and You will take care of me in due time according to Your will. In Jesus' name. Amen.*

# 7
## "BUT THEY DID NOT CONSULT THE LORD..."

*Suggested Scripture reading: Joshua 9*

Think of the last time you needed to make an important decision. Perhaps you wrote out a pros and cons list, or called a few friends for advice. You considered the various outcomes of the decision and what seemed best for you and your family. You may have even consulted the Bible (obviously a good thing). But did you pray?

The Israelites were in the process of claiming the Promised Land as their own. They defeated Ai in the second battle, after Ai originally defeated them due to Achan's sin as discussed previously. After this victory, Joshua took the time to remind the Israelites of the blessings and curses spelled out in the book of instruction, as well as every word of every command.

Joshua was following through with God's earlier instructions for success:

> "Be strong and very courageous. Be careful to obey all the law my servant Moses gave you; do not turn from it to the right or to the left, that you may be successful wherever you go. Keep this Book of the Law always on your lips; medi-

tate on it day and night, so that you may be careful to do everything written in it. Then you will be prosperous and successful" (Joshua 1:7-8).

It seemed Joshua had consulted the Lord in all he did. Until he didn't.

The Gibeonites had heard what the Israelites had done to Ai and Jericho, and Joshua 9:4 says "they resorted to deception to save themselves" (NLT).

They put on worn-out clothing and carried with them moldy bread, so it appeared they had been on a long journey. When they requested an alliance be formed, "the Israelites said to the Hivites, 'But perhaps you live near us, so how can we make a treaty with you?'

'We are your servants,' they said to Joshua.

But Joshua asked, 'Who are you and where do you come from?'" (Joshua 9:7-8).

The Gibeonites said they had come from a very distant country. They had heard of the Israelites' God and of all He did in Egypt, at the Jordan, and Jericho and Ai. "This bread was hot from the ovens when we left our homes. But now, as you can see, it is dry and moldy. These wineskins were new when we filled them, but now they are old and split open. And our clothing and sandals are worn out from our very long journey" (Joshua 9:12-13, NLT).

Here is how Joshua responded: "So the Israelites examined their food, but they did not consult the Lord" (Joshua 9:14, NLT).

Sometimes in my life, I ignore the most obvious first step – talking to God about the choice I'm facing. This was not the case in my early days of walking with Jesus. I seemed to know very deeply in those first steps of following Him how desperate my need for Him was. These days, I can be more likely to stress out about it and wrestle mentally with what is the right way to go. If it seems like a less important decision, I might just quickly think about it and choose.

I love how simply Philippians 4 puts it: "Don't worry about anything; instead, pray about everything. Tell God what you need, and thank him for all he has done. Then you will experience God's peace, which exceeds anything we can understand. His peace will guard your hearts and minds as you live in Christ Jesus (verses 6-7, NLT)." Certainly, worrying is not the answer. Handing the situation over to God and trusting Him to guide and direct me is.

As recorded in Joshua 7, when God didn't come through as Joshua expected, he immediately fell on his face before the Lord. Until evening, he cried out to God, asking what went wrong. Yet when he was faced with the Gibeonites' deceit just a short time later, he stared at the supposed evidence instead of lifting his eyes to the Lord.

Proverbs states, "There is a way which seems right to a person, but its end is the way of death" (14:12, NASB). Joshua made a treaty with the Gibeonites, thinking they lived far away, only to find out they lived *in* the Promised Land. Joshua kept his word and upheld the treaty but lost part of the land that should have been inherited by the Israelites. Even centuries later, God upheld this treaty, as recounted in 2 Samuel 25. King Saul had put some of the Gibeonites to death, and his successor King David had to make a heartbreaking decision to avenge this wrong (2 Samuel 25:1, 5-6).

Jesus told His disciples the importance of remaining in Him, and staying connected to Him as their source. He summarized this idea in John 15:5 by stating frankly, "Apart from Me, you can do nothing."

I need to ask myself: am I missing out on God's promises and blessings because I forget to stop and ask God to inform my decisions?

Do I say "yes" to opportunities that appear to have God-glorifying potential because it seems like a "good" thing to do?

Or do I ask for God's input every time I prepare to take a step in any direction?

It seemed good to Joshua to make a treaty with these people. But the Bible clearly states he didn't stop to ask God's opinion. As has been said earlier in this book, the "good" can be the enemy of God's best.

*Prayer: Lord, forgive me for often acting without asking. Help me remember You in every step, even every small move I make. Let the weight of "Apart from me you can do nothing" convict me and inform every decision, especially my choice to pray. Help me trust that You are good and able to guide and direct me into all truth, through the Holy Spirit. In Jesus' name I pray. Amen.*

## 8

## THE STRENGTH OF CALEB

*Suggested Scripture reading: Joshua 14*

My father was diagnosed with cancer in 2000. He was expected to live only a few years, something he chose not to tell me. My father had not made a profession of faith in Jesus at that time. He would state that while he was Christian, he was not a born-again Christian, and that he believed all paths lead to God. My prayer to God (more like my demand!) during those early years was always that God would keep my dad alive long enough for him to declare Jesus Lord of his life.

Watching my father get sick reminded me that there are so many things in life that are outside of our control, especially matters of health. I decided one of the best ways to live a long, strong, fruitful life for Jesus is to do what I can to control what I can. Since coming to this realization, I've tried to do what I can to live a healthy lifestyle. This hit home even harder when I was diagnosed with a chronic illness at the end of 2018 (though I had been symptomatic for about seven years at that time). Though I've always been active (walking, biking, and frequenting the gym for other forms of exercise), I had never been consistent in using weights. One thing I've done to combat the progression of this condition is to lift weights, beginning to seriously strength training in early 2021.

Caleb was 40 years old when he and Joshua with ten others initially scouted out the promised land. Caleb and Joshua were the only two spies who had the faith to believe God would give them victory. Scripture states that Caleb is now 85 years old (Joshua 14:10). Two-and-a-half tribes had settled east of the Jordan, so the rest of the land needed to be divvied up. The tribe of Judah (Caleb's tribe) approached Joshua at Gilgal (Joshua 14:6). Before the lots were cast to give each tribe their allotment of land, Caleb spoke up.

Caleb reminded Joshua of Moses' promise, when Moses said to Caleb that "because [Caleb had] followed the Lord my God wholeheartedly," Caleb would get the land on which he had walked at this point 45 years ago (Joshua 14:9). Caleb told Joshua, "I am still as strong today as the day Moses sent me out; I'm just as vigorous to go out to battle now as I was then. Now give me this hill country that the Lord promised me that day. You yourself heard then that the Anakites were there and their cities were large and fortified, but the Lord helping me, I will drive them out just as he said" (Joshua 14:11-12).

The Anakites are historically considered to be giants, based on Deuteronomy 2:10, 21; 9:2. Perhaps this was why that part of the Promised Land had not yet been conquered. Yet at 85 years old, Caleb seemingly had no hesitation in taking them on. Now, imagine the patience it took to wait 45 years to see God's promise come to fruition. Imagine the daily choice to trust God. Imagine the care Caleb must have taken to remain strong so that when the time came, he would be able to do his part in walking in the fullness of all God had for him.

I do a good amount of reading and listening in the area of fitness, health, and wellness. On a podcast episode touching on these topics, the host had undergone quite a physical transformation by losing a significant amount of weight as well as participating in body building. She said something to the effect of how she hopes when she walks down the street, people will look at her and think, *Don't mess with her!*[1]

Did Caleb do lots of push-ups, sprint up-and-down maintains, and bench press logs to keep strong? We can't know that for sure, of course. Did he remind himself of God's laws, so that he could remain focused on following the Lord wholeheartedly? Did he maintain a healthy distance from the grumblers and complainers, so that his sole focus remained on God? This we can assume to some degree to be true. But whatever Caleb had done to be ready in all areas, to stay alive long enough to live in the fullness of the Promised Land, we see the result: "Then Joshua blessed Caleb son of Jephunneh and gave him Hebron as his inheritance. So Hebron has belonged to Caleb son of Jephunneh the Kenizzite ever since, because he followed the LORD, the God of Israel, wholeheartedly" (Joshua 14:13-14).

It is recorded in Judges 1:20, "Then they gave Hebron to Caleb, as Moses had promised; and he drove out from there the three sons of Anak." Even after the death of Joshua, Caleb was still going strong! I imagine Caleb, climbing those hills to fight the Anakites, and them thinking, *I don't want to mess with him!* And all because of "the LORD helping" him (Joshua 14:12).

I hope this will be the case for me as well. About two years ago, I was on the phone with someone, being interviewed for a life insurance policy. They had concerns about my diagnosis. The interesting thing was that the agent interviewing me was very familiar with my condition. In fact, her mother had the same thing! She seemed shocked when I told her I've never missed a day of work because of it. I attribute that both to God's faithful and my perseverance in strength training since early 2021 (and still going strong).

I can also gratefully report that God answered my prayer for my father, keeping him alive far longer than those few years he was expected to live. Twelve years after his diagnosis, my dad made that profession of faith in Christ, living at least eight more years than was initially predicted.

Like Caleb, we must maintain our own physical, emotional and spiritual strength, so that with God's help, we can be prepared for whatever life bring.

*Prayer: Lord, help us to remain sharp in all areas of life. Help us care for our bodies and our health in a way that honors You. Let us steward our emotions, so that You will be glorified in all we do, say, or think. I commit to reading and meditating on Your Word regularly, so that I will continually be transformed by the renewing of my mind (Romans 12:1-2). I recommit my whole self to You, as a living sacrifice. May my life always honor You. In Jesus' name I pray. Amen.*

## 9
## GOD'S SPECIFIC PLAN

*Suggested Scripture reading: Joshua 13-15, 19*

I recently had an interesting conversation with a group of friends about whether or not God has a specific plan for our lives. It seems many were brought up in a generation that was very focused on uncovering your specific "plan and purpose" for which God created you. Having prayed for years while hoping to discern this purpose, some had given up on finding it.

Reading the later chapters of Joshua can get a little tedious. It's a long list of the town names and valley names and which tribe got what land - and it goes on and on and on. After all, there were 12 tribes, and an estimated one million people!

But as I read, I can't help but think about how specific God's plan is. He spelled it out for them. It was His job to make His plan clear, not their job to somehow locate it.

I understand the type of frustration my friends shared. I used to kill myself trying to find God's plan. I'd get on my knees and tell God I wasn't moving until He spoke to me and told me everything I wanted to know about my future.

Then, one day, in May of 2004 while teaching at a student ministry conference, He spoke. Here is part of what He said.

*"I do have a plan for you – a wonderful plan that will shock, delight and surprise you, a plan that will blow your small ambitions out of the water."* He then went on to tell me I wasn't ready to hear about that plan.

This was *not* what I expected God to say.

What God went on to speak to my heart that day was that I needed to be still and experience Him as God (Psalm 46:10), that He is so different than any other relationship I've ever known. He called me to climb up into His lap and allow Him to change me, to lean back and rest my head against His heart, so I might know and experience all the wonderful things He feels for me.

God's primary desire was not to "use" me, as in have me do great things; He primarily wanted to change me. I simply needed to let Him love me. His goal for me in that time was to deposit in my heart His love, the new identity He died to give me, and His vision for my wholeness.

It's amazing to look back on that time in my life, and see what God has done in the many years since. When I look at His children now, I wish I could somehow give some of what God has deposited into my heart (His deep and passionate love for each of us, His tender care and compassion, His desire to see us walk in freedom and live overflowing lives) and transplant it into someone else's heart. I now do this little by little, bit by bit, through teaching, writing, blogging, and my current project of weekly "Coffee with Brenna" videos. I would not be able to do that now if I hadn't allowed God to work in me for all the years since 2004.

Let me be clear. I absolutely believe God has a specific plan for each of His children who call Him by name. But we can kill ourselves (and kill our faith) trying to "find" it.

Jesus said my sheep hear my voice (John 10:27, KJV). Period, end of story. The God who spoke the whole world into existence can make His voice heard by you when you need to hear it *and* if you are open to hearing it.

Every day, this becomes more challenging. Between our addiction to staring at our phones and the volume of the many voices on social media, we have conditioned ourselves to be continually entertained. In order to hear God speaking, we need to be willing to silence the other voices and be still, as God spoke to me in 2004.

God does not give us a road map with an "X" marking the spot. It would be easier in some ways if He did, but then we wouldn't have to trust in Him and cling to Him so tightly; we'd simply have to trust in the map.[1]

I don't want to get to know a map. I want to purpose to know my Creator, the One who shaped me and formed me and laid out my life.

I'm not going to argue over whether or not God literally maps out every minute of every day. What I do know is that God created each of us with gifts and talents, passions and desires, that He wants to use in specific ways.

We love to quote Jeremiah 29:11 in situations like this: "'For I know the plans I have for you,' declares the LORD, 'plans to prosper you and not to harm you, plans to give you hope and a future'" (Jeremiah 29:11). However, as a friend of mine pointed out, the context for this verse is the exile that occurred hundreds of years after the book of Joshua takes place, after the kings of Israel fail to follow the Lord. Jeremiah 29:11 is God's promise of goodness to the Israelites after decades of captivity and exile.[2]

The book of Joshua is full of promises concerning God's plans for the Israelites as they too left the captivity of Egypt and the wanderings of the wilderness. Clearly, they were also plans for prosperity and hope. These specific plans would come to fruition if the people continued to follow God with their whole hearts and grew to know Him more and more.

God will reveal His plans to us as well if we continue to

cling to Him and strive to know Him. Rather than strive to find "the map" of specific plans, it's been much healthier (as the friends mentioned above have also realized) for me to just follow Him. I follow His commands and teachings, love Him and continually surrender to Him, dream, and make the time and space to listen for His voice. I keep living life while doing those things, rather than looking for a sign from heaven or always seeking after the next big thing. In the midst of that, as I cling to God, read His Word and spend time with His people, God will show me what He has for me.

*Prayer: Lord, I want to know Your will for my life. I long to know Your specific plan. More than that, Lord, I want to know You. As Paul prayed, I want to primarily know Christ crucified, and the power of Your resurrection. I want to experience the overflowing life Jesus died to give me. I want everything in my life to be grounded in the truth that I am Your beloved, I belong to You, and I am Yours. Help me to seek You and to trust that You will reveal Your plan to me in due time. In Christ's name I pray. Amen.*

## 10

## EMBRACE DISCOMFORT

*Suggested Scripture reading: Joshua 17-18*

In 2012, we made a huge change in our lives.

We were living in Boston. I had lived there for 15 years at that point, and my husband had basically lived in the greater Boston area his whole life. As I mentioned previously, my dad had been sick for over 11 years and was likely going to die. Virginia, where my father lived, felt so very far away.

So we took a big step of faith. My husband quit his job. We started getting our condo ready to sell, so we could move to Virginia.

In the midst of that, I felt God calling me to run a marathon and raise money for a cause for which I was deeply passionate. I kept thinking that because God called me to register for the race, it would get easier. I'd get faster. Maybe I'd even get that "light and fresh feeling" that runners talk about.

I had some issues with my legs, possibly due to the chronic illness with which I had yet to be diagnosed. Sometimes when I ran, they felt like lead. They never really felt good. I had a hope that God would heal them while I was running and that He would be glorified in how quickly and effortlessly I finished.

Well, God did not heal my legs while I ran. Though I started off strong, I kept getting slower and slower. My stomach revolted. My body screamed at me for 20 of the 26.2 miles.

After that marathon, we moved into temporary housing in Virginia. We needed to secure an apartment, find jobs, and get settled into life there.

Three weeks later, my father died.

This was not how I thought it would happen. I uprooted my family because I envisioned at least months together. I hoped that my sons would have the opportunity to get to know my dad better, and I could spend quality time with him after living 500 miles apart for 14 years.

I couldn't help but wonder, *Did we make the right decision?*

Joshua 10-12 chronicles all of God's victories through the Israelites and the land that was conquered. Two-and-a-half tribes had settled east of the Jordan, but some of the land to the west still needed to be won. Joshua 13-17 lists which tribe would inherit which part of the land still unconquered.

Throughout this time, we see signs of the Israelites getting comfortable and complacent.

> "Yet the Manassites were not able to occupy these towns, for the Canaanites were determined to live in that region. However, when the Israelites grew stronger, they subjected the Canaanites to forced labor but did not drive them out completely" (Joshua 17:12-13).

The people of Joseph asked for more land but then complained that the people they would have to defeat "have chariots fitted with iron" (Joshua 17:16).

Sound familiar?

What happened? They crossed the Jordan, conquered Jericho, and cleared out cities. At one point, the sun and moon stood still, so they could win a battle (Joshua 10:12-14). Perhaps they no longer saw the need to do the hard work of driving out those living in the Promised Land?

By Joshua 17, there were still seven tribes who had not received their inheritance.

> "So Joshua said to the Israelites: 'How long will you wait before you begin to take possession of the land that the Lord, the God of your ancestors, has given you?'" (Joshua 18:3).

"Has given." Every translation I looked at put it the same way. God has already done it. Now it was time to walk out that truth.

As part of our transition to Virginia, I left the ministry that God had allowed me to shape over the course of the previous 9.5 years; it had also shaped me. As I spoke to my dear friends at Alive in Christ at what I thought would be my last weekly meeting, I remembered something.

Often we must embrace discomfort in order to be obedient. We must embrace discomfort to get to the Promised Land. I wrote about this in the earlier section "Stepping into your Jordan." I wrote about it years ago in an article called "Craving Egypt."[1]

The Israelites did not want to embrace the discomfort of continuing to conquer the Promised Land.

After all, they had scorned discomfort during their wilderness journey every time an obstacle came up, even when they just got hungry or thirsty. Egypt had the discomfort of slavery, but at least it was a familiar discomfort. Yeah, they might have been slaves, but there was meat to eat there, not this miracle bread from heaven!

The Promised Land was scary. There were giants there, rivers at flood stage, and towns with high walls around them. They had already fought so many battles – wasn't that enough?

As I spoke to my wonderful "perseverers" at Alive in Christ that night, I reminded them (and myself) that sometimes we need to embrace the pain of discomfort in order to take hold of all God has for us.

Once again, the Israelites had another opportunity to see, trust, and go and take hold.

*Prayer: Lord, I don't want to wander aimlessly in the wilderness for decades when the journey need only take two weeks. I want all You have for me. Help me to trust, to step out and to take hold of Your hand as You guide and lead me. Help me to embrace discomfort, believing that the Promised Land is on the other side. Help me to know, deep in my heart, that You are good and that You surround me with Your mercy, strength, and love. For it is in Your name I pray. Amen.*

# 11

## NO OTHER GODS

*Suggested Scripture reading: Joshua 23*

The space had been divided; the Israelites had received their inheritance. They were settling into their new homes. It's exciting to imagine the Israelites in the Promised Land!

In chapter 23, we hear Joshua imploring the leaders and elders of the Israelites to continually follow God with everything they have.

> "So be very careful to follow everything Moses wrote in the Book of Instruction. Do not deviate from it, turning either to the right or to the left. Make sure you do not associate with the other people still remaining in the land. Do not even mention the names of their gods, much less swear by them or serve them or worship them. Rather, cling tightly to the Lord your God as you have done until now" (v. 6-8, NLT).

In Joshua 24 (which we will consider more fully in the next section), God implored all of Israel to "throw away the gods your ancestors worshiped beyond the Euphrates River and in Egypt, and serve the Lord" (v. 14b).

No other gods.

When we think about "other gods" or idols, we often think about the golden calf that the Israelites melted their jewelry to create (Exodus 32). Perhaps we think about statues of Buddha and maybe even some of the things we read about later in the Bible, like Asherah poles.

How do we apply Joshua's admonition to the Israelites into our modern-day context? What do idols look like today?

Here are some examples of things we worship or things we run after that impede putting God first:

- The god of money or career or possessions – sacrificing quality time with friends and family to get ahead, get more "stuff" or try and save for the future.
- The god of entertainment or distraction – spending more time on your phone or streaming shows than you spend with God or in building relationships.
- The god of sex or relationships – believing the lie that sex, marriage, or romantic attachment will meet my deepest needs.[1]
- The god of appearances – deep down, fearing being vulnerable with people because you care too much about what people think, or fearing you will be abandoned if you are honest.[2]
- The god of comfort – staying right where we are because it is familiar and comfortable rather than risking surrender to God.[3]

How do we discern if we might have idols in our lives? Here are some questions to test for idolatry[4]:

- What do I value?
- What do I strive for and dream of the most?
- What has most of my time and attention?
- What ideas or drives am I most loyal to following?
- What do I think about most of the time?
- What am I unwilling to question? Are there areas of my life or even my personality that I say, "That's just how it is," or "It's just who I am"?
- Am I so attached to certain things (personal property, career paths, promotions, my phone) that other areas of my life and growth are clearly hindered?
- Are there areas of my life that I am unwilling (or feel unable) to surrender to God?

The Israelites had an amazing opportunity here. They were in the Promised Land. God had fought their battles and cleared a spacious place for them to live in peace. All they had to do was leave behind their idols and follow Him with their whole hearts.

No other gods.

What would they choose? You can read Judges and beyond to find out. The more important question is this: what will you choose?

*Prayer: Jesus, what does it look like in my life for me to serve other gods today? What is holding me back from choosing You and fully surrendering to You? Am I overfocused on what I can see, so much so that I struggle to choose to trust in You? Do I feel unable to go and take hold of all you have for me in Your specific plan for me? Lord, I desperately need Your help. I need Your empowerment and discernment. I declare that even though I know I will do this imperfectly, I choose to throw aside anything I put above You in my life, anything I chase after harder than You. God, I pick You. Help me to walk that out fully and wholeheartedly so I might thrive in the*

*Promised Land, so that I might experience that overflowing life that Jesus died to give. For it is in His precious, powerful, mighty, healing, comforting name I pray, Amen.*

## 12

## CHOOSE FOR YOURSELF

*Suggested Scripture reading: Joshua 24*

One of the first Bible study series I was part of as a young believer was a video series called "Choices."[1] The full name of the series is "Choices: To Be or Not to Be a Woman of God." The series was so impactful to me for several reasons. First, Alicia Britt Chole (the presenter) mentioned a woman who struggled with same-sex attraction who walked away from the Lord to embrace a gay identity. I had never heard anyone in the church talk about this topic before. Second, she broke down walking with Jesus into choice after choice after choice. That made perfect sense to me. It's just one step at a time, one foot in front of the other, one day at a time.

In the final chapter of Joshua, God shares through Joshua His plan for the Israelites. He starts as far back as Terah, the father of Abraham, and how their ancestors worshipped other gods when they lived beyond the Euphrates River. God through Joshua reminds them how He sent Moses and Aaron to be His vessels in bringing them out of the slavery they were experiencing in Egypt. Though they lived in the wilderness a long time, God brought then to the land of the Amorites, where they fought and had victory. He carried them to the Jordan, where they stepped out in faith, and on to Jericho, where a string of victories began (v. 2-13).

Joshua went on to say, "But if serving the Lord seems undesirable to you, then choose for yourselves this day whom you will serve, whether the gods your ancestors served beyond the Euphrates, or the gods of the Amorites, in whose land you are living. But as for me and my household, we will serve the Lord" (Joshua 24:15).

The Israelites seemed to recognize that God had carried them to this point. They saw what could happen if they disobeyed God (Achan and the defeat at Ai), or if they didn't consult him (the treaty with the Gibeonites). They seemed to acknowledge that the reason they had been able to conquer the Promised Land was that God had empowered and equipped them to do so. But what would they do now?

Alicia Britt Chole talks about a pivotal time in her life when she and her husband found out they could not bear children together. After hearing this heartbreaking news, they began to pursue adoption. When they found out the adoption would cost more than their annual missionary salary, Alicia sat down at the piano and wrote this song.

> WHAT WOULD HAPPEN *if I really believed*
> *You were the God with Whom*
> *Nothing is impossible?*
> *What would happen if I really believed*
> *That You were good?*
> *Where would fear and doubt go?*
> *And what could happen if Your Church,*
> *Chose to take You at Your Word,*
> *United by Your precious Name,*
> *Called upon You*
> *And then stood to proclaim (that)*

*We believe that God is good*
*We believe His Word is true*
*We believe He never fails*
*We believe His love prevails*
*We believe He will provide*
*We believe He's by our side*
*We believe He still forgives*
*We believe that Jesus lives!*[2]

WHAT WOULD HAPPEN? How would our lives change if we choose to believe the fullness of all God is?

My journey of freedom, this journey to and into the Promised Land, began with choosing to believe God is who He says He is. It began with recognizing the lies I had believed, about myself and about God, and learning to think like a free person in order to fully walk in the freedom Jesus died to give.[3]

Choice after choice after choice – will we choose to follow God with our whole hearts or not? Choose to throw away those other goods – or not? Choose to believe that He is good and faithful and loving and with us – or not?

We cannot skip this step. We will not be able to see with God's eyes, trust in His ability, and go and take hold through His power without first choosing for ourselves whom we will serve. These three steps are contingent upon and empowered by following God wholeheartedly.

So today, friends, as we wrap up the book of Joshua, we are faced with a choice.

"But if serving the Lord seems undesirable to you, then choose for yourselves this day whom you will serve, whether the gods your ancestors served beyond the Euphrates, or the gods of the Amorites, in whose land you are living. But as for me and my household, we will serve the Lord (Joshua 24:15)."

Choose for yourself. But choose today.

*Prayer: God, I can easily see that I haven't always made the best choices. I can also see there have been times when I have sworn wholeheartedly, as the Israelites did in Joshua 24, that I would serve You and You alone. But then I quickly strayed, just as they did. As the old song says, I am prone to wander.[4] But today, Lord, I will serve You. I choose You – right now, this minute. Lord, help me to do it again every hour until tomorrow, and then help me to do it again. You have been so good to me. In the name of Your Son who You allowed to be crushed for me I pray, Amen.*

# AFTERWORD: HIS TREASURED POSSESSION

*Suggested Scripture reading: Deuteronomy 7:1-11*

What is your most treasured possession? The thing that the last time you moved, you put in your car instead of the moving truck? Or when you needed to pack it away for some reason, you took great care in doing so?

The book of Deuteronomy is one long admonition from Moses to the Israelites. It is directly before the book of Joshua. While this story is not in Joshua, the words in this book set the stage for what is to come.

The Israelites would soon be entering the Promised Land. Since Moses could not go with them, there were some things he wanted them to remember. In the midst of warnings not to intermarry, cautions not to bring detestable things into their new homes, reminders to not forget God, and encouragements to not be afraid, we find this gem:

> "For you are a people holy to the Lord your God. The Lord your God has chosen you out of all the peoples on the face of

the earth to be his people, his treasured possession" (Deuteronomy 7:6).

This passage is an echo of what God told Moses at an earlier time to share with the Israelites:

> "'You yourselves have seen what I did to Egypt, and how I carried you on eagles' wings and brought you to myself. Now if you obey me fully and keep my covenant, then out of all nations you will be my treasured possession. Although the whole earth is mine, you will be for me a kingdom of priests and a holy nation.' These are the words you are to speak to the Israelites.'" (Exodus 19:4-6).

In speaking of this passage in Exodus, Henry T. and Richard Blackaby say this, "Three months after they left Egypt, God reminded His people why He had delivered them 'on eagles' wings.' It was to bring the people to Himself. That is, God saved them so that they could enjoy intimate fellowship with Him."[1]

Written at the end of forty years of wandering, it would be easy for the reader of Deuteronomy to become overly focused on Moses' numerous warnings of "Don't do this, do this, and don't do this." Sometimes I know I get overly focused on those things myself. But we must not lose sight of the "why."

God had chosen the Israelites. He called them by name and set them apart to know Him intimately. He absolutely treasured them. Just like a good parent instructs a child to look both ways before he crosses the street, God counseled the Israelites on these do's and don'ts because He didn't want to see them harmed.

I have a few treasured possessions myself. I remember specifically is a piece of driftwood that belonged to my father. When my family and I moved back to New England after living in Virginia for 20 months, I carefully wrapped that driftwood in a blanket. My dad saved that unique piece of wood because it reminded him of a dancer. While packing, it was padded on the sides to insure nothing bumped into it or damaged it. If someone else were to move it, I would call out, "Be careful!" because it is just that important to me.

I chose to include this section in the book because after reading all of these chapters about God's amazing plan for your life and the promised land He has for you, you may still have doubts. Perhaps you struggle with believing you have worth, or that your life has meaning. This was a struggle for me as well. This is why this section is so important.

You matter to God. Stop for a moment and say it out loud: I matter to God. He took the time to create you and give you life. He loves you. You may only see your flaws and mistakes, but God sees you as so much more than that – as His treasure. Take a moment to let that soak in. He encourages us and admonishes us to grasp the "life that is truly life" (1 Timothy 6:19), an abundant life that will satisfy us so much more fully than anything else (John 10:10). Because His love is better than life (Psalm 63:3). Because He delights in us (Psalm 18:19).

The Israelites needed this encouragement as they headed to the Promised Land. Joshua did as well. Twice, Moses is told by God to encourage Joshua (Deut. 1:38, 3:28). They needed to be reminded that God was going to take care of them if they chose to walk in His ways.

He will take care of us as we commit ourselves to Him because we too are His treasured possession.

*Prayer: Lord, I don't always look at myself as Your treasure. In fact, as I pray that, I realize perhaps I never thought of myself that way. Lord, as I go about my days, as I see things in my life that I cherish and handle with care – my children, my family, my friends, even some things I own – let me be reminded that You feel that way about me, except much, much more! Holy Spirit, who is truth, guide me into all truth (John 16:13). Breathe life into this truth; make it come alive in my heart and be evidenced in my life. Let me be reminded that Your Law serves to protect me, not to take away my freedom, for true freedom is found in Jesus Christ alone. I pray in His Name. Amen.*

# ACKNOWLEDGEMENTS

I began to write a series on my blog from the book of Joshua in 2011.[1] I quickly fell in love with this book of the Bible, so much so my daughter, born in 2014, has the middle name "Jordan."

This book could not have happened without the love, prayers, and support of so many. Here are a few of those people.

Special thanks:

To the ladies at Brockton Assembly of God, for participating in the first test run study of "Lessons from Joshua" on Zoom during the height of COVID-19,

To Rev. Dr. R. Steven Warner, for answering all of my initial theological questions on the book of Joshua,

To Dr. Hugh Rutledge, for giving thoughtful yet positive feedback on the near-final product in terms of theology and history,

To so many others for your general cheerleading of my writing and my weekly "Coffee with Brenna" YouTube videos[2],

To my children, Nathanael, JJ, and Maggie, who are all stones of remembrance of God's faithfulness,

To my husband, Roy, for not only designing the cover but believing in me,

To my Heavenly Father, who called me by name in January, 1999, and reminded me in October, 2020, "Joshua 3 is your faith story. I will always ask you to do hard things." Every day, God gives me opportunities to step into the Jordan at flood stage. And I wouldn't have it any other way.

# NOTES

### Background

1. Gordon J. Wenham, *Numbers: An Introduction and Commentary*, vol. 4 of Tyndale Old Testament Commentaries. IVP/Accordance electronic ed. (Downers Grove: InterVarsity Press, 1981), 131. Matthew Henry, *Commentary on the Whole Bible (Unabridged)*, Accordance electronic ed. (Altamonte Springs: OakTree Software, 2004), paragraph 3863.

### 1. See. Trust. Go & Take Hold.

1. "Go Up and Possess It." https://blackaby.org/go-up-and-possess-it/ Accessed 5/9/2024.
2. A book I have not read but was recommended to me is "Show Them No Mercy: Four Views on God and Canaanite Genocide" edited by Stanley Gundry. I will warn you - it is very scholarly! My NIV1984 "The Student Bible" (unfortunately out of print) has a very helpful explanation on pages 248-249. The more recent NIV Study Bible (copyright 2020) also has an article covering this on pages 338-339.

### 2. Stepping into Your Jordan

1. Jon Krakauer, *Into the Wild* (United State, Anchor Books, 1997).
2. John Ortberg. If You Want to Walk on Water, You've Got to Get Out of the Boat. Pg. 80, http://www.johnortberg.com/the-water-or-the-boat/

### 3. Stones of Remembrance

1. https://languages.oup.com/google-dictionary-en/
2. https://www.boundless.org/faith/craving-egypt/

### 4. Seeing with God's Eyes

1. The males born in the wilderness as well as those who had not initially been on military age had not been circumcised. This is explained more thoroughly in Joshua 5:4-8.
2. Richard S. Hess, *Joshua: An Introduction and Commentary*, vol. 6 of Tyndale Old TestAment Commentaries. IVP/Accordance electronic ed. (Downers Grove: InterVarsity Press, 1996), 140.

I found the Tyndale Commentary to be extremely insightful on this portion of scripture, so much so that I was tempted to copy and paste it in its entirety. At the time of this printing, I could not find a free version online.
3. Matthew Henry, *Commentary on the Whole Bible (Unabridged)*, Accordance electronic ed. (Altamonte Springs: OakTree Software, 2004), paragraph 5540.

Matthew Henry Concise Commentary is available for free here: https://www.christianity.com/bible/commentary/matthew-henry-concise/joshua/5

## 5. When Life Doesn't Make Sense

1. https://utmost.org/the-good-or-the-best/

## 6. Trust God to Care for You

1. My friend and theologian Hugh Rutledge points out that first fruits and tithes should not be confused. In our current economy, first fruits would be giving all of your first paycheck, whereas tithes would be 10% on the rest.

## 8. The Strength of Caleb

1. I don't have the exact episode, but this is the podcast: https://www.nobsweightloss.com/podcast/ Be warned; she swears quite a bit.

## 9. God's Specific Plan

1. Many might say at this point that God did give us a map; it's the Bible. And that is correct! The Bible, however, is the living and active Word which directs our overall actions and decisions. In this case, I am speaking of specific direction on our unique calling and purpose that comes not only from reading His Word but also from hearing God's voice and the guidance of the Holy Spirit.
2. Thank you, Hugh Rutledge, for this reminder and the insight it brings!

## 10. Embrace Discomfort

1. https://www.boundless.org/faith/craving-egypt/

## 11. No Other Gods

1. A concept from the book *Relational Masks* by Russell Willingham.
2. If you would like to read more on this topic, see the book *Relational Masks* by Russell Willingham.
3. Read more about the fear of the unknown here: http://www.livingunveiled.com/2011/12/02/freedom-friday-fear-of-the-unknown/
4. https://churchplants.com/articles/6455-the-top-7-gods-americans-worship.html mixed with some of my own thoughts

## 12. Choose for Yourself

1. https://aliciachole.com/product/choices-woman-god/
2. Used with permission, Dr. Alicia Britt Chole, www.aliciachole.com. © *Alicia Britt Chole, 1997 used with permission of onewholeworld, inc.*
3. This is discussed more thoroughly in my 1st book, *Learning to Walk in Freedom*, but you can watch a video from June 5, 2020 on my YouTube channel for a primer. The video is entitled "Think Like a Free Person."
4. The hymn is "Come, Thou Fount of Every Blessing," public domain.

## Afterword: His Treasured Possession

1. "God Brings You to Himself," https://blackaby.org/god-brings-you-to-himself/ Accessed 5/9/2024.

## Acknowledgements

1. www.livingunveiled.com is my blog address.
2. www.youtube.com/@BrennaKateSimonds